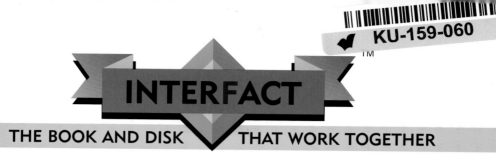

INTERFACT ™

THE BOOK AND DISK THAT WORK TOGETHER

WEATHER

TWO CAN ™

CHANHASSEN, MINNESOTA • LONDON

www.two-canpublishing.com

Published by Two-Can Publishing,
18705 Lake Drive East, Chanhassen, MN 55317

www.two-canpublishing.com

© Two-Can Publishing 2000, 1998
Text copyright © Miranda Bower

Created by
act-two
346 Old Street
London EC1V 9RB

ISBN 1-85434-901-5

2 4 6 8 10 9 7 5 3

A catalogue record for this book is available from the British Library

Photograph credits: Robert Harding Picture Library/Warren Faidley: front cover; Bruce
Coleman: p.8, p.9 (t), p.14 (bl), p.16, p.24 (bl), p.26, p.28, p.29 (tl); Steve Davey: p.27 (t);
Frank Lane Picture Agency: p.22 (bl); NHPA: p.19 (t); Oxford Scientific Films: p.17,
p.18 (t), p.22 (t), p.24 (t); Planet Earth Pictures: p.18 (b); Science Photo Library:
p.10 (l), pp14–15, p.31; Zefa: p.9 (r), p.13, p.20, p.25 (t), p.32 (br), p.33 (bl), p.33 (tl)

Every effort has been made to acknowledge correctly and contact the source of each
picture and Two-Can Publishing apologises for any unintentional errors or omissions
which will be corrected in future editions of this book.

Printed in Hong Kong by Wing King Tong

INTERFACT

INTERFACT will have you hooked in minutes —
and that's a fact!

⬤ **The disk is packed with interactive activities, puzzles, quizzes and games that are fun to do and packed with interesting facts.**

If you've got a question about the weather, just ask Wallace and Wilma.

What makes thunder and lightning?

Click on Wilma for the answer or click on Wallace to ask another question

⬤ **Open the book and discover more fascinating information highlighted with lots of full-colour illustrations and photographs.**

How do forecasters predict the weather? Read up and find out!

To get the most out of **INTERFACT**, use the book and disk together. Look out for the special signs, called Disk Links and Bookmarks. To find out more, turn to page 43.

23

BOOKMARK

DISK LINK
Do you know why clouds form? Just ask Wilma in WEATHER WISE.

Once you've clicked on to **INTERFACT**, you'll never look back.

LOAD UP!
Go to **page 40** to find out how to load your disk and click into action.

What's on the disk

HELP SCREEN

Learn how to use the disk in no time at all.

Welcome to the
INTERFACT
disk on Weather

To have a look at all the different things on the disk, simply click the arrow keys with your mouse.

As you do this, you'll see a description of each activity in the reading box.

Click on the picture at the top of the screen to select the activity you want to investigate.

Get to grips with the controls and find out how to use:

- arrow keys
- reading boxes
- 'hot' words

THE HEAT IS ON

Find out why planet Earth could be about to lose its cool!

Take a closer look at global warming. Use your mouse to build an interactive picture on screen and discover why greenhouse gases could be turning up the heat.

UP, UP AND AWAY

Release a weather balloon and watch it float away.

Altitude : 9km
Temperature : −38.5°C
Pressure : 280mb

Follow a weather balloon as it floats up into the sky. Learn about the layers of the atmosphere, take a look at different types of cloud and find out where the weather is made.

MADE TO MEASURE

Check out the tools used to measure the weather!

A drought is a long period without rain.

See how different weather conditions affect different weather instruments. Watch what happens to a thermometer, a barometer, an anemometer, a rain gauge – and a piece of seaweed!

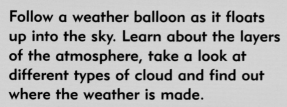

WORLD OF WEATHER

Investigate some of the wildest weather in the world!

Join weather woman Gail Force and explore the most amazing weather around the world. Learn about stupendous storms, fabulous fogs – and showers of maggots!

WEATHER WISE

All your weather questions answered!

How do clouds form? What is lightning? To get some straight answers to these and lots more weather questions, just ask Wallace and Wilma.

QUICK AS A FLASH!

Are you a weather wizz? Find out in this quiz!

A cute kitten is stuck in a tree and a huge thunderstorm is brewing. Summon the fire brigade by answering questions all about weather and rescue the poor puss before the downpour.

MELTDOWN

Save the snowman with your knowledge of weather words!

Use the lingo you've learned in the book and disk to save the snowman. The sun is coming up and he's starting to melt. You'll have to think fast or he'll turn into a puddle!

What's in the book

*All words in the text that appear in **bold** can be found in the glossary*

Weather world

What is weather? It is the cold or warm, wet or sunny conditions that affect our planet. What we wear, what we eat and where we live depends on the weather around us.

▶ The world is divided into different areas of weather zones. The zones differ depending on how close they are to the **Equator**, how far they are from the coast, and how high the land is.

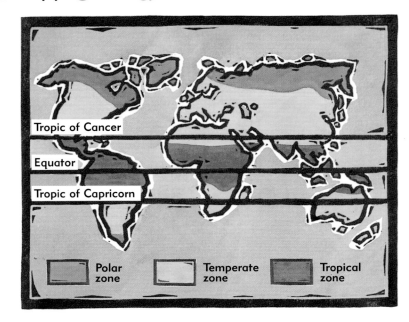

Tropic of Cancer

Equator

Tropic of Capricorn

Polar zone   Temperate zone   Tropical zone

▲ Without heat from the Sun, our world would be cold, lifeless and frozen. The amount of sunshine we receive depends on where we are on the planet.

◀ The science of weather is called meteorology. It comes from 'meteoron', a Greek word meaning 'talking about the heavens'. Scientists who study the weather are called meteorologists. They make observations from weather stations, like this one at the North Pole.

The Sun is the most important part of our weather. Not only does it warm the land, it also helps to create rain, fog and snow. It does this by drawing up moisture into the air from oceans, lakes and rivers.

▲ When a layer of air is heated by the Sun's rays, it becomes lighter and rises. Cooler, heavier air rushes in to take its place and a wind is formed. Some parts of the world have very strong winds. **Hurricanes** are one of the most violent types of wind. They form over the warmest parts of the world's oceans.

Sky watch

Did you hear the **weather forecast** today? How does a meteorologist know what the weather is going to be like? Forecasts are made by studying information collected at weather stations around the world. This information comes from instruments that are carried in planes, satellites, ships – and even balloons!

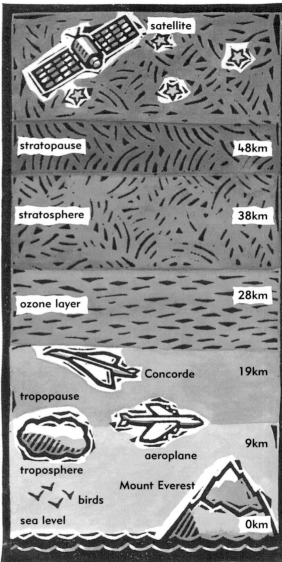

▲ This computer picture of a **hurricane** was built up from signals beamed to the Earth from a weather satellite. Satellites are useful because they collect information that cannot be seen from the ground, such as cloud patterns over a wide area. Computers in weather stations plot the information on a map to produce a picture of the weather. These pictures can also show **temperature** and rainfall.

satellite

stratopause   48km

stratosphere   38km

28km

ozone layer

Concorde   19km

tropopause

9km

aeroplane

troposphere   Mount Everest

birds

sea level   0km

▲ The Earth is surrounded by a layer of gases, called the **atmosphere**, that protects us from extremes of temperature. All weather develops in the troposphere, the layer closest to the Earth.

◀ Weather balloons float high into the atmosphere. They carry radio probes that transmit details of the temperature and the **humidity** of the air. These signals are collected by weather stations.

▼ Satellites circle, or orbit, the Earth from outside the atmosphere. Their orbits vary from about 250km to more than 35,000km above the Earth.

DISK LINK
Release a weather balloon and follow it through the atmosphere in UP, UP AND AWAY.

POP

▼ There are natural ways of forecasting weather. Seaweed becomes damp and limp when rain is due but is crisp and dry in sunny weather. Also, pine cones open when it is warm but stay closed on cold days.

Round and round

DISK LINK
Remember the weather words
you pick up in this chapter.
What you learn may help you
save the day in MELTDOWN.

Hang out wet clothes on a warm, breezy day and before long they are dry. This is because of **evaporation**. The water has changed into **vapour** – droplets in the air that are so tiny you cannot see them. The air around you always contains water vapour – even if you are in a desert!

▶ On some farms in Australia, water is stored in open tanks covered by floating, white, plastic balls. Rain collects in the tanks but the sunshine reflects off the balls. As a result, less water evaporates and so less water is lost.

▼ Put the Aussie farmers' trick to the test and see if it works. Pour equal amounts of water into two identical containers. Cover the surface of the water in one container with polystyrene beads. Leave both containers in a sunny spot that is protected from the wind. After several days, measure the water from each container.

▲ In the cold of night, some water vapour forms **condensation** and settles as drops of dew, shown above. As the Sun comes up, the air gets warmer and the dew evaporates.

Heavens above

Watching the clouds is a good way to predict what the weather is going to be like. Fluffy, white clouds are common in summer and rarely bring rain. If dark clouds cover most of the sky, then rain is likely to fall.

▲ Fog is a cloud that lies close to ground level. It often forms on still, cool mornings.

▼ Try making a cloud in a bottle. Ask an adult to fill a jar with hot water. Leave it to stand for a moment, then pour most of it away. Put some ice cubes on a piece of thin material, stretched over the top of the jar. Where the warm and cold air meet, a small cloud forms.

▲ **Cumulonimbus clouds** bring thunderstorms and heavy showers of rain.

▲ Even in fine weather, wispy **cirrus clouds** can mean that rain is due.

▲ Thick, flat **stratus clouds** can produce overcast weather and often bring drizzle.

DISK LINK
Do you know why clouds form? If the answer is no, just ask Wilma in WEATHER WISE.

Rain drain

Rain is part of the **water cycle**. The Sun's heat creates **vapour** by drawing up water from oceans, seas, rivers and lakes. As the vapour rises and meets cold air, it forms droplets that come together to make clouds. When the droplets become heavy enough, they fall as rain. The water drains into rivers, lakes, seas and oceans and the cycle begins again.

The water cycle

▲ When the tiny water droplets in a cloud collide they join together to form larger drops of rainwater. A raindrop may contain about one million cloud droplets before it is heavy enough to fall.

▼ Fill a jar with water and place it on a sunny window sill. Put a piece of white paper next to the jar so that you see bright colours reflected on it. The water in the jar splits the sunlight into the seven colours of the **rainbow**.

If there is a shower while the Sun is still shining, the individual raindrops can split the light of the Sun into an arc of coloured bands called a rainbow. The bands always appear in the same order of red, orange, yellow, green, blue, indigo and violet.

DISK LINK
Take a good look at this picture. You might be asked a question about rainbows in QUICK AS A FLASH.

Floodgates

Heavy rains may cause floods. Rivers can swell during rainstorms and overflow their banks. Water then floods the surrounding land.

► Sometimes, valleys are flooded on purpose when a **dam** is built across one end. A **reservoir** of water forms behind it. The force of the water rushing through holes in the dam is sometimes used to make electricity.

◄ A sudden flood can ruin crops, destroy homes and take lives.

► Make a rain gauge. Fit a funnel into the neck of a jar and put it outside to collect rainwater. Pour the water into a measuring jug and compare how much rain falls each day.

DISK LINK
Look at how different weather conditions affect a rain gauge in **MADE TO MEASURE**.

▶ Flooding is not always bad news, as long as people are warned in time. In many parts of the world, such as on this farm in Brazil, rivers break their banks during each rainy season. The waters carry particles of rock, worn away from the river bed. When the water finally drains away, valleys are left covered in a rich mud that is good for growing crops.

Howling winds

Wind is the movement of air. It can be as gentle as a breeze or as violent as a **hurricane**.

▼ A tornado forms when warm air rises rapidly and is replaced by more warm air. Air is sucked up, forming a huge tunnel that spins very quickly.

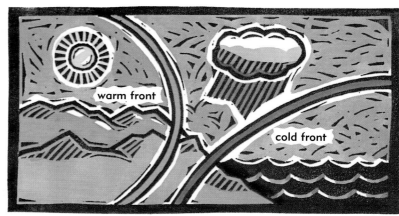

warm front

cold front

◀ Air can be cold, warm, damp or dry, depending on the land or sea below it. Warm air rises and cold, heavy air rushes in to take its place, making a wind. The edges of large masses of air are called **fronts**. Clouds and rain often form where cold and warm fronts meet.

▶ In 1805, Admiral Sir Beaufort invented a scale to measure wind speed at sea. This version was for use on land.

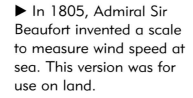

◀ To make a **weather vane**, tape paper arrow shapes to the ends of a straw. Ask an adult to pin it to a stick or pencil. Push the stick through the bottom of a large yogurt pot. Use a compass to mark North, South, East and West. Fix the pot with modelling clay in a level, windy place.

DISK LINK
Do you know where the windiest place on Earth is? You'll find out in **WORLD OF WEATHER**.

THE BEAUFORT SCALE

0 **Calm:** No movement.

1 **Light air:** Weather vanes stay still, smoke drifts in the air.

2 **Light breeze:** Wind felt on face, weather vanes move, leaves rustle.

3 **Gentle breeze:** Leaves and twigs move, flags flap.

4 **Moderate breeze:** Small branches sway, dust and paper blow about.

5 **Fresh breeze:** Small trees sway, small waves form on water.

6 **Strong breeze:** Large branches sway, hard to use an umbrella.

7 **Moderate gale:** Large trees sway, difficult to walk against the wind.

8 **Fresh gale:** Twigs snap off trees.

9 **Strong gale:** Slates blow off roofs.

10 **Whole gale:** Trees are uprooted, buildings are damaged.

11 **Storm:** Widespread damage.

12 **Hurricane:** Violent destruction.

Thunder and lightning

Meteorologists look out for heavy rain, strong winds and **thunder** so that they can send out storm warnings. This means that people can take steps to protect their homes and property.

▼ This charred tree was scorched by lightning. Storms damage trees and buildings every year.

▲ Lightning is caused by a giant build-up of **static electricity** inside a thunder cloud Eventually, the electricity bursts out as a bolt of lightning. Because it takes the fastest route to Earth, lightning often strikes tall buildings and trees.

▶ Many modern buildings are fitted with metal strips called lightning conductors. They lead lightning safely to the ground.

Static electricity causes lightning – but that's not all! You can see it in action in other ways, too. Rub a balloon on your clothes and then press it against a smooth wall. Static electricity will make the balloon cling to the wall.

DISK LINK
When a balloon pops, the air moves so quickly that it makes a bang. Thunder is caused in the same way. Find out more in WEATHER WISE.

Snow and ice

In very cold air, water **vapour** inside clouds turns into tiny crystals of ice. As the crystals bump into one another, they join up and become snowflakes.

▲ **Hailstones** form in **cumulonimbus** clouds. Frozen raindrops move about in the cloud, gathering layers of ice. When hail is heavy enough, it falls. The biggest ever hailstone was the size of a bowling ball!

▲ Sometimes, droplets in water vapour freeze on to surfaces such as window panes. They form patterns of ice crystals, called **frost**.

◄ Snowflakes form when ice crystals in cold clouds freeze together. When you look at snowflakes through a magnifying glass, you'll see that, although each one has six points, no two snowflakes are the same.

DISK LINK
Use your knowledge
of cool weather words
to stop the snowman
melting in MELTDOWN.

▲ A layer of snow acts like a blanket and protects plants and seeds from harsh frost. Many animals go into **hibernation** during the winter. Sheep grow thick, woolly coats to keep them warm during the cold months.

Do not use a glass bottle. It might break!

▶ Fill a plastic bottle to the top with water. (Make sure it is plastic and not glass.) Screw the lid on tight and put the bottle in the freezer. After a while, the bottle will bulge and crack. This is because water expands when it freezes – which is why water pipes sometimes burst in cold weather.

Heat and drought

Droughts occur when there is much less rain than usual. In a severe drought, animals and people can die. It becomes difficult to grow crops because the soil turns to dust and is blown away.

▶ The world's desert regions are dry all year round. However, crops can be grown in an **oasis**, or in areas where **irrigation** is used.

DISK LINK
Weather woman Gail Force has some hot facts about deserts in **WORLD OF WEATHER**.

◀ In the desert, a year's supply of rain may fall in a single downpour. Some desert plants grow and flower very quickly.

▶ Make your own sundial! Cut out a large circle from a piece of card. Then cut out a right-angled triangle with a flap. Fold back the flap and glue it to the circle as shown. Go outside and use a compass to line up the sundial on a North-South line. Each hour, mark where the shadow falls on the circle.

◀ Aeroplanes often fly above cloud level. The sky is always clear there, even if it is raining below.

▶ **Thermometers** measure temperature using the **Celsius** or **Fahrenheit** scales. As the temperature rises, the liquid at the bottom of the thermometer expands and rises up the tube.

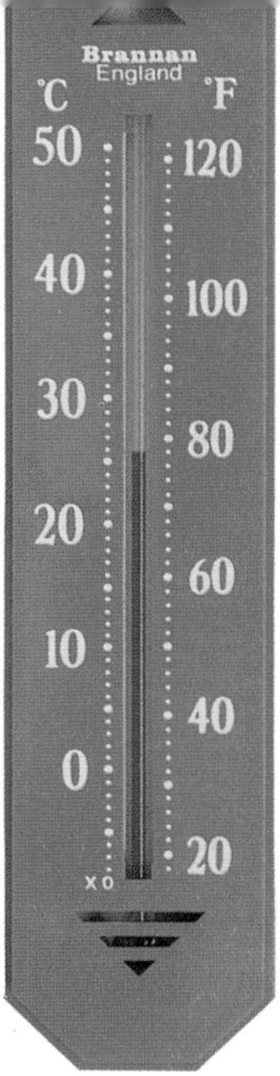

Brannan
England

°C   °F
50   120
40   100
30   80
20   60
10
           40
0
           20
x 0

Changing weather

The Earth is surrounded by a layer of gas called the **atmosphere**. The atmosphere includes a gas called carbon dioxide. This gas helps to keep our planet at the correct temperature.

◄ Our **climate** changes slowly, over time. However, scientists now think that the way we live is affecting the balance of the gases in the atmosphere. This imbalance could mean that our climate changes more quickly.

▼ Trees use carbon dioxide to make energy. As we destroy forests, more of this gas builds up in the atmosphere. This could cause major weather changes.

DISK LINK
The world's weather seems to be hotting up. Do you know why? Find out in **THE HEAT IS ON.**

◀ Air **pollution** can turn raindrops into acid! Car exhausts, factories and power stations pump waste gases out into the air. Some of these gases mix with water **vapour** in clouds to produce acid, which falls as rain. This polluted rainwater damages the environment. Acid rain poisons rivers and lakes. It kills trees and even eats away at the stonework on buildings.

▶ Is there acid rain where you live? Try this experiment to find out. Ask an adult to boil half a red cabbage in water. Leave it to soak for several hours, then strain the liquid into a dish. Soak some strips of white blotting paper in the juice and let them dry. Now take three of the strips you have made and dip one into the juice of a lemon, dip another into some tap water and dip the third one into some rainwater. The stronger the acid in the liquid, the pinker your testing strip will be.

Simple seasons

Have you ever wondered why different parts of the world have different patterns of cold and warm weather throughout the year?

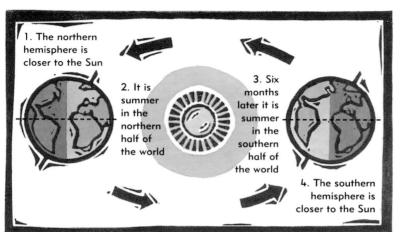

1. The northern hemisphere is closer to the Sun

2. It is summer in the northern half of the world

3. Six months later it is summer in the southern half of the world

4. The southern hemisphere is closer to the Sun

▲ The Earth orbits the Sun once a year, spinning as it goes. The **seasons** change as the different **hemispheres** of the Earth tilt towards or away from the Sun. Temperate regions of the world have four seasons: spring, summer, autumn and winter. Tropical areas, near the Equator, are hot all year round but they may still have two seasons – a dry one and a rainy one.

DISK LINK
Temperate and tropical are two of the different types of climate. To learn about the others, ask Wilma in WEATHER WISE.

◄ People change habits with the seasons. In winter, we wear layers of clothing to trap heat. In summer, we wear sunglasses and loose clothing and use skin lotions to protect us from the Sun.

▲ Some animals travel to warm regions to escape the cold of the winter months. This is called **migration**. These monarch butterflies travel 3,000km every year from North to South America.

The weather and you

The weather affects us all in different ways – often more than we realise. Changing seasons can affect our moods and feelings too. Sunny, warm weather makes many people feel much happier than cold, wet weather.

▼ On summer days, many people suffer from hay fever. This is caused by the pollen that is produced by flowers.

▲▼ We play different sports in different seasons. Swimming is a popular activity during the summer and many people ski in the winter.

DISK LINK
Remember what you read on this page. It could help you avoid a catastrophe in QUICK AS A FLASH!

◄ Climate may affect the type of building we choose to live in. Houses in hot countries, such as Greece, are often painted white to reflect the sun. They may also have small windows to keep the heat out. But in cool countries, many of the houses have **double-glazed** windows to keep the heat in.

▲ ► Surveys show that windy, stormy weather often makes people grumpy. Some illnesses seem to get worse in bad weather. For example, chest complaints are more painful on a cold or foggy day.

Glossary

Atmosphere is the layers of different gases that surround the Earth.

Celsius is a scale used to measure temperature.

Cirrus clouds are thin and wispy and are made up of ice particles.

Climate is the pattern of weather in a region.

Condensation is when water vapour cools and changes back into a liquid.

Cumulonimbus clouds are tall with a dark, grey underside.

Dam is a barrier of concrete or earth, built across a river or valley.

Double-glazed windows have two panes of glass that trap air and help to keep the warmth inside a house.

Sun   Rain cloud

Droughts are long periods during which little or no rain falls in an area.

Equator is the imaginary line around the centre of the Earth.

Evaporation is the process that changes water from a liquid into a gas.

Fahrenheit is a scale used to measure temperature.

Front is the boundary between two different air masses.

Frost is dew or water vapour that has frozen to form ice particles. It often forms at night, on objects that are out of doors.

Hailstones are small balls of ice that fall from cumulonimbus clouds.

Hemisphere is one half of the Earth. The Earth is divided in half along the Equator.

Hibernation is the long period of inactivity, similar to sleep, that some animals go into during the winter months.

Humidity is the amount of moisture in the air.

Hurricanes are the strongest type of stormy winds.

Irrigation is a method of channelling water into areas where there is little rain and the soil is dry.

Migration is when animals travel around the world at different times of the year.

Oasis is an area in a desert where water and, often, vegetation are found.

Pollution is caused by harmful chemicals that poison the water, soil or air.

Rainbows are bands of multicoloured light created when sunlight shines through raindrops.

Reservoir is an artificial lake, created by people rather than by nature.

Seasons are patterns of weather that occur at different times of the year.

Static electricity is the energy created when certain materials rub together.
Stratus clouds are flat, layered clouds

that are often grey in colour.

Temperature is a measure of how hot or cold something is. It is usually measured in degrees Fahrenheit (°F) or Celsius (°C).

Thermometer is an instrument used for measuring temperature.

Thunder is the loud bang created when the air inside a cloud suddenly expands.

Vapour is an invisible gas in the air. Water changes from a liquid to a vapour when it is heated.

Water cycle is the movement of water between the Earth and the atmosphere. Water on the Earth evaporates, forms clouds and returns to the Earth again as rain, hail or snow.

Weather forecast is a prediction of what the weather will be like in the future.

Weather vane is an instrument used to show wind direction.

Work book

Work book

Photocopy this sheet and use it to make your own notes.

Loading your INTERFACT disk

INTERFACT is easy to load. But, before you begin, quickly run through the checklist on the opposite page to ensure that your computer is ready to run the program.

Your INTERFACT CD-ROM will run on both PCs with Windows and on Apple Macs. To make sure that your computer meets the system requirements, check the list below.

SYSTEM REQUIREMENTS

PC/WINDOWS
- Pentium 100Mhz processor
- Windows 95 or 98 (or later)
- 16Mb of RAM (24Mb recommended for Windows 98)
- VGA 256 colour monitor
- SoundBlaster-compatible soundcard
- 1Mb graphics card
- Double-speed CD-ROM drive

APPLE MACINTOSH
- 68020 processor (PowerMac or G3/iMac recommended)
- System 7.0 (or later)
- 16Mb of RAM
- Colour monitor set to at least 480 x 640 pixels and 256 colours
- Double-speed CD-ROM drive

LOADING INSTRUCTIONS

You can run INTERFACT from the CD – you don't need to install it on your hard drive.

PC WITH WINDOWS 95 OR 98

The program should start automatically when you put the disk in the CD drive. If it does not, follow these instructions.

1 Put the disk in the CD drive
2 Open MY COMPUTER
3 Double-click on the CD drive icon
4 Double-click on the icon called WEATHER

PC WITH WINDOWS 3.1 OR 3.11

1 Put the disk in the CD drive
2 Select RUN from the FILE menu in the PROGRAM MANAGER
3 Type D:\WEATHER (Where D is the letter of your CD drive)
4 Press the RETURN key

APPLE MACINTOSH

1 Put the disk in the CD drive
2 Double-click on the INTERFACT icon
3 Double-click on the icon called WEATHER

CHECKLIST

● Firstly, make sure that your computer and monitor meet the system requirements as set out on page 40.

● Ensure that your computer, monitor and CD-ROM drive are all switched on and working normally.

● It is important that you do not have any other applications, such as wordprocessors, running. Before starting INTERFACT quit all other applications.

● Make sure that any screen savers have been switched off.

● If you are running INTERFACT on a PC with Windows 3.1 or 3.11, make sure that you type in the correct instructions when loading the disk, using a colon (:) not a semi-colon (;) and a back slash (\) not a forward slash (/). Also, do not use any other punctuation or put any spaces between letters.

How to use INTERFACT

INTERFACT is easy to use.
First find out how to load the program
(see page 40) then read these simple
instructions and dive in!

You will find that there are lots of different features to explore. Use the controls on the right-hand side of the screen to select the one you want to play. You will see that the main area of the screen changes as you click on to different features.

For example, this is what your screen will look like when you play The Heat Is On – where you create a picture and learn about global warming. Once you've selected a feature, click on the main screen to start playing.

Click on the arrow keys to scroll through the different features on the disk or find your way to the exit.

Click here to select the feature you want to play.

Click to continue

This is the reading box where instructions and directions appear explaining what to do. Go to page 4 to find out what's on the disk.

DISK LINKS

When you read the book, you'll come across Disk Links. These show you where to find activities on the disk that relate to the page you are reading. Use the arrow keys to find the icon on screen that matches the one in the Disk Link.

DISK LINK
Look at how different weather conditions affect a rain gauge in MADE TO MEASURE.

BOOKMARKS

As you play the features on the disk, you'll bump into Bookmarks. These show you where to look in the book for more information about the topic on screen. Just turn to the page of the book shown in the Bookmark.

23

WORK BOOK

On pages 36–39 you'll find note pages to photocopy and use again and again. Use them to write down your own discoveries as you go through the book and the disk.

HOT DISK TIPS

- After you have chosen the feature you want to play, remember to move the cursor from the icon to the main screen before clicking on the mouse again.

- If you don't know how to use one of the on-screen controls, simply touch it with your cursor. An explanation will pop up in the reading box!

- Keep a close eye on the cursor. When it changes from an arrow → to a hand ☞ click your mouse and something will happen.

- Any words that appear on screen in blue and are underlined are 'hot'. This means you can touch them with the cursor for more information.

- Explore the screen! There are secret hot spots and hidden surprises to find.

Troubleshooting

If you have a problem with your INTERFACT disk, you should find the solution here. You can also e-mail for help at helpline@two-canpublishing.com.

QUICK FIXES Run through these general checkpoints before consulting COMMON PROBLEMS (see opposite page).

QUICK FIXES

PC WITH WINDOWS 3.1 OR 3.11

1 Check that you have the minimum specification: (see PC specifications on page 40).

2 Make sure you have typed in the correct instructions: a colon (:) not a semi-colon (;) and a back slash (\) not a forward slash (/). Also, do not use punctuation or put any spaces between letters.

3 It is important that you do not have any other programs running. Before you start **INTERFACT**, hold down the Control key and press Escape. If you find that other programs are open, click on them with the mouse, then click the End Task key.

QUICK FIXES

PC WITH WINDOWS 95 or 98

1 Make sure you have typed in the correct instructions: a colon (:) not a semi-colon (;) and a back slash(\) not a forward slash (/). Also, do not use punctuation or put any spaces between letters.

2 It is important that you do not have any other programs running. Before you start **INTERFACT**, look at the task bar. If you find that other programs are open, click on them with the right mouse button and select Close from the pop-up menu.

APPLE MAC

1 Make sure that you have the minimum specification: (see Apple Macintosh specifications on page 40).

2 It is important that you do not have any other programs running. Before you start **INTERFACT**, click on the application menu in the top right-hand corner. Select each of the open applications and select Quit from the File menu.

COMMON PROBLEMS

Symptom: Cannot load disk.
Problem: There is not enough space available on your hard disk.
Solution: Make more space available by deleting old applications and programs you are not using.

Symptom: Disk will not run.
Problem: There is not enough memory available.
Solution: *Either* quit other applications and programs (see Quick Fixes) *or* increase your machine's RAM by adjusting the Virtual Memory.

Symptom: Graphics do not load or are of poor quality.
Problem: *Either* there is not enough memory available *or* you have the wrong display setting.
Solution: *Either* quit other applications and programs (see Quick Fixes) *or* make sure that your monitor control is set to 256 colours (MAC) or VGA (PC).

Symptom: There is no sound (PCs only).
Problem: Your sound card is not Soundblaster compatible.
Solution: Configure sound settings to make them Soundblaster compatible (see your sound card manual for more information).

Symptom: Your machine freezes.
Problem: There is not enough memory available.
Solution: *Either* quit other applications and programs (see Quick Fixes) *or* increase your machine's RAM by adjusting the Virtual Memory.

Symptom: Text does not fit neatly into boxes and 'hot' words do not bring up extra information.
Problem: Standard fonts on your computer have been moved or deleted.
Solution: Re-install standard fonts. The PC version requires Arial; the Mac version requires Helvetica. See your computer manual for further information.

Index